JOHN

Prison Book Project
PO Box 592
Titusville, FL 32781

REFORMED EXPOSITORY BIBLE STUDIES

A Companion Series to the Reformed Expository Commentaries

Series Editors

Daniel M. Doriani
Iain M. Duguid
Richard D. Phillips
Philip Graham Ryken

1 Samuel: A King after God's Own Heart
Esther & Ruth: The Lord Delivers and Redeems
Song of Songs: Friendship on Fire
Daniel: Faith Enduring through Adversity
Matthew: Making Disciples for the Nations (two volumes)
Luke: Knowing for Sure (two volumes)
John: The Word Incarnate (two volumes)
Galatians: The Gospel of Free Grace
Ephesians: The Glory of Christ in the Life of the Church
Philippians: To Live Is Christ
Hebrews: Standing Firm in Christ
James: Portrait of a Living Faith

JOHN

THE WORD INCARNATE

Volume 2 (Chapters 11–21)

A 13-LESSON STUDY

REFORMED EXPOSITORY
BIBLE STUDY

JON NIELSON
and **RICHARD D. PHILLIPS**

P&R
P U B L I S H I N G
P.O. BOX 817 • PHILLIPSBURG • NEW JERSEY 08865-0817

Scripture quotations are from the ESV® Bible (The Holy Bible, English Standard Version®), copyright © 2001 by Crossway, a publishing ministry of Good News Publishers. Used by permission. All rights reserved.

All boxed quotations are taken from Richard D. Phillips's John, vol. 2, in the Reformed Expository Commentary series. Page numbers in quotations refer to that source.

The quoted material at the end of the boxed quotation on page 112 is from James Montgomery Boice, The Gospel of John, vol. 5, Triumph through Tragedy: John 18–21 (Grand Rapids: Baker Books, 1999), 1654.

ISBN: 978-1-62995-930-6 (pbk)
ISBN: 978-1-62995-931-3 (ePub)

Printed in the United States of America

CONTENTS

SERIES INTRODUCTION

Studying the Bible will change your life. This is the consistent witness of Scripture and the experience of people all over the world, in every period of church history.

King David said, "The law of the LORD is perfect, reviving the soul; the testimony of the LORD is sure, making wise the simple; the precepts of the LORD are right, rejoicing the heart; the commandment of the LORD is pure, enlightening the eyes" (Ps. 19:7–8). So anyone who wants to be wiser and happier, and who wants to feel more alive, with a clearer perception of spiritual reality, should study the Scriptures.

Whether we study the Bible alone or with other Christians, it will change us from the inside out. The Reformed Expository Bible Studies provide tools for biblical transformation. Written as a companion to the Reformed Expository Commentary, this series of short books for personal or group study is designed to help people study the Bible for themselves, understand its message, and then apply its truths to daily life.

Each Bible study is introduced by a pastor-scholar who has written a full-length expository commentary on the same book of the Bible. The individual chapters start with the summary of a Bible passage, explaining **The Big Picture** of this portion of God's Word. Then the questions in **Getting Started** introduce one or two of the passage's main themes in ways that connect to life experience. These questions may be especially helpful for group leaders in generating lively conversation.

Understanding the Bible's message starts with seeing what is actually there, which is where **Observing the Text** comes in. Then the Bible study provides a longer and more in-depth set of questions entitled **Understanding the Text**. These questions carefully guide students through the entire passage, verse by verse or section by section.

It is important not to read a Bible passage in isolation, but to see it in the wider context of Scripture. So each Bible study includes two **Bible Connections** questions that invite readers to investigate passages from other places in Scripture—passages that add important background, offer valuable contrasts or comparisons, and especially connect the main passage to the person and work of Jesus Christ.

The next section is one of the most distinctive features of the Reformed Expository Bible Studies. The authors believe that the Bible teaches important doctrines of the Christian faith, and that reading biblical literature is enhanced when we know something about its underlying theology. The questions in **Theology Connections** identify some of these doctrines by bringing the Bible passage into conversation with creeds and confessions from the Reformed tradition, as well as with learned theologians of the church.

Our aim in all of this is to help ordinary Christians apply biblical truth to daily life. **Applying the Text** uses open-ended questions to get people thinking about sins that need to be confessed, attitudes that need to change, and areas of new obedience that need to come alive by the power and influence of the Holy Spirit. Finally, each study ends with a **Prayer Prompt** that invites Bible students to respond to what they are learning with petitions for God's help and words of praise and gratitude.

You will notice boxed quotations throughout the Bible study. These quotations come from one of the volumes in the Reformed Expository Commentary. Although the Bible study can stand alone and includes everything you need for a life-changing encounter with a book of the Bible, it is also intended to serve as a companion to a full commentary on the same biblical book. Reading the full commentary is especially useful for teachers who want to help their students answer the questions in the Bible study at a deeper level, as well as for students who wish to further enrich their own biblical understanding.

The people who worked together to produce this series of Bible studies have prayed that they will engage you more intimately with Scripture, producing the kind of spiritual transformation that only the Bible can bring.

Philip Graham Ryken
Coeditor of the Reformed Expository Commentary series

INTRODUCING JOHN

The gospel of John is one of the world's true treasures. It contains many of the sayings that are most memorable and blessed to God's people. The book is so simple that children memorize their first verses from its pages and so profound that dying adults ask to hear it as they pass from this life. It is said that John is a pool safe enough for a child to wade in and deep enough for an elephant to drown in. Martin Luther wrote, "This is the unique, tender, genuine, chief Gospel. . . . Should a tyrant succeed in destroying the Holy Scriptures and only a single copy of the Epistle to the Romans and the Gospel according to John escape him, Christianity would be saved."[1]

Although this gospel does not specify its **author**, we can be sure of his identity from both internal and external evidence. The book claims to be written by an eyewitness and disciple of Jesus (21:24). We know from the other gospels that the disciples closest to Jesus were Peter, James, and John. Of these, only John is never named in this gospel—which is hard to explain apart from the author's modesty concerning himself. In his place we are told of a "beloved disciple" who is evidently both the author and the apostle John. The early church affirms this view. Irenaeus, a second-century bishop who knew people who had personally known John, attests that John, "the disciple of the Lord," wrote this gospel in Ephesus, and his view is backed up by every ancient document that addresses the subject.[2]

We do not know the exact **date** when John wrote his book. It is traditionally thought to be the last of the four gospels to be composed. Some

1. Quoted in James Montgomery Boice, *The Gospel of John*, vol. 1, *The Coming of the Light: John 1–4* (Grand Rapids: Baker Books, 1999), 13.
2. Irenaeus, *Against Heresies*, 3.1.1, trans. W. H. Rambaut, in *The Apostolic Fathers with Justin Martyr and Irenaeus*, The Ante-Nicene Fathers 1, ed. A. Cleveland Coxe (repr., Peabody, MA: Hendrickson, 1999), 414.

scholars place its writing before the destruction of the temple in AD 70. But the consensus holds that John wrote it no earlier than AD 80 and perhaps as late as the AD 90s.

Although we must surmise the gospel's author, its **main purpose** is clearly stated: "These are written so that you may believe that Jesus is the Christ, the Son of God, and that by believing you may have life in his name" (20:31). John is sometimes called the "gospel of belief," because it was written to inspire faith in Jesus and his gospel. Specifically, it tells us that we are to believe that "Jesus is the Christ, the Son of God" and also that, through faith in him, we receive "life in his name." Given this statement of purpose, we may approach the gospel of John as especially communicating these two precious themes.

The first **theme**—the gospel of John's overwhelming presentation of Jesus as the Son of God—makes it widely recommended to those who are looking for an introduction to the Christian faith. Its opening lines refer to Jesus as "the Word" who in the beginning was "with God" and "was God" (1:1). Then, toward the end of the book, the disciple Thomas believes and falls before Jesus, after his resurrection from the dead, crying, "My Lord and my God!" (20:28). In between these two poles, the book presents numerous claims of Jesus's deity. John's prologue in chapter 1 describes Jesus's incarnation in terms of Isaiah 7:14's promise regarding *Immanuel* ("God with us"): "The Word became flesh and dwelt among us, and we have seen his glory, glory as of the only Son from the Father, full of grace and truth" (1:14). Joined with John's teaching about Jesus's deity is his equal insistence on the doctrine of the Trinity, since Jesus is "the only God, who is at the Father's side" and "has made him known" (1:18).

After John's prologue comes what scholars refer to as the "Book of Signs" (1–11), which consists largely of Jesus's miracles. These further display his deity. Jesus turns water into wine in John 2; performs miraculous healings in John 4, 5, and 9; feeds more than five thousand people with a few loaves and fish, then walks on water, in John 6; and raises Lazarus from the grave in John 11. His claim to deity brings him into conflict with the religious authorities, which leads him to make even clearer statements regarding his divine nature. For instance, when Jesus tells the Jewish leaders, "Before Abraham was, I am" (8:58), he deliberately takes God's most sacred self-revelation and applies it to himself (see Ex. 3:14).

John's gospel is known for its seven famous "I am" sayings. Jesus associates his ministry with God's gift of manna to Israel in the desert: "I am the bread of life" (6:35). He sets himself forth as the true source of divine blessing: "I am the light of the world" (9:5). He is "the door" (10:9), "the good shepherd" (10:11), "the resurrection and the life" (11:25), "the way, and the truth, and the life" (14:6), and "the true vine" (15:1). These claims are clear and bold, and by them we learn how Jesus brings God's saving grace to a world that is lost in sin.

Connected to the theme of Jesus's divinity is the idea that he is "the Christ." The Greek word *Christos* is a translation of the Hebrew *Meshuach*: the long-awaited Messiah of God's people. This word means "anointed one" and refers to the three anointed offices that Jesus came to fulfill: prophet, priest, and king.

- Jesus is the true prophetic revelation of God's being and character. By his gracious nature, righteous deeds, and saving words, Jesus reveals God to all the world: "Whoever has seen me has seen the Father" (14:9).
- Jesus also comes as the true King of God's people, in the line of his earthly father, David. When the Roman governor Pontius Pilate claims authority over Jesus, Jesus replies to him, "My kingdom is not of this world" (18:36)—referring to the kingdom of heaven.
- Jesus comes as the Priest who cleanses believers from their sins by offering himself as their true atoning sacrifice. The second main portion of John's gospel, known as the "Book of the Passion" (12–21), records the events surrounding Jesus's crucifixion and his glorious resurrection from the grave.

Jesus the Christ fulfills the work of the prophets by revealing God through his own life. He restores kingly rule over God's redeemed people, and he ministers as the true Priest by shedding his own blood, just as John the Baptist predicted (see 1:29).

If the first part of John's purpose is to persuade us that Jesus is "the Christ, the Son of God," the second part, and second theme, is to show that we receive eternal life through personal faith in Jesus. The most well-known verse in John—and perhaps the whole Bible—eloquently states this gospel truth: "For God so loved the world, that he gave his only Son, that whoever believes in him should not perish but have eternal life" (3:16). The appeals that the book contains about taking up personal faith in Jesus start with Jesus's call to his disciples in John 1. After Jesus's first miracle, we read that "his disciples believed in him" (2:11). Jesus says that "the Son of Man [must] be lifted up [on the cross], that whoever believes in him may have eternal life" (3:14–15). God the Father invests Jesus with the authority to save, and so Jesus declares, "Whoever hears my word and believes him who sent me has eternal life. He does not come into judgment" (5:24). Again and again, John connects personal faith in Jesus to forgiveness of sins and eternal life.

In addition to the themes of Jesus's deity and our salvation through faith, John includes additional content that is absent from Matthew, Mark, and Luke. In particular, the early chapters of his gospel provide more scenes from Jesus's ministry of evangelism, as the Savior calls disciples to trust and follow him. John provides new information about Jesus's calling of the disciples and follows it with his nighttime encounter with the Pharisee Nicodemus, during which Jesus tells him, "You must be born again" (3:7). Particularly uplifting is Jesus's saving encounter with an unnamed woman by a well, whom Jesus offers the "living water" of spiritual life (4:10; see also v. 14). When the woman believes, she immediately tells the people of her village about Jesus, and they too believe. Like this woman, readers are motivated and instructed to spread the gospel by Jesus's command at the book's conclusion: "As the Father has sent me, even so I am sending you" (20:21).

Further new material consists of Jesus's Farewell Discourse in John 13–16, followed by his High Priestly Prayer in John 17. In these chapters, John provides great detail about Jesus's last meal with his disciples on the night of his arrest. After humbly washing their feet, Jesus discusses at length the provision of the Holy Spirit after Jesus has departed from the world. In John 17, one of the most remarkable and informative chapters of the entire Bible, Jesus prays to the Father for his church as he stands on the brink of surrendering himself to the cross. As we listen to the Son of God praying for us, we stand like Moses on holy ground, filled with astonished adoration as Jesus's love for our souls is revealed.

As do Matthew, Mark, and Luke, John narrates the details of Jesus's atoning death and glorious resurrection, but this book again provides a wealth of material that is not found elsewhere. The world, in all its malice, conducts a false trial to legitimize Jesus's murder. Pilate, who represents the authority of man's kingdom, cynically consigns Jesus to death despite his clear innocence. Jesus is presented to the Jewish crowd in a "crown of thorns and [a] purple robe" (19:5)—in mockery of his divine claims—and Pilate affixes a sign to his cross that reads, "Jesus of Nazareth, the King of the Jews" (v. 19). As Jesus dies on the cross for our sin, he cries aloud glorious words of victory—"It is finished" (v. 30)—before giving up his life. After he rises from the grave on the third day, he meets with Mary Magdalene and "doubting" Thomas, among others, to present them with his resurrection body. The book concludes with Jesus's tender pastoral ministry to Simon Peter, as he graciously gives him the commission "Feed my sheep" (21:17).

Countless readers have discovered the truth about Jesus and his gospel in the pages of John. It is, in fact, Jesus himself whom we meet in this book, through the ministry of God's Holy Spirit and the words of inspired Scripture. Jesus himself promises you that if you believe in him and read this gospel in faith, "you will know the truth, and the truth will set you free" (8:32).

Richard D. Phillips
Coeditor of the Reformed Expository Commentary series
Coeditor of the Reformed Expository Bible Study series
Author of *John* (REC)

LESSON 1

THE RESURRECTION AND THE LIFE

John 11:1–57

THE BIG PICTURE

As we begin our study of the second half of John's gospel, we come to a pivotal (and glorious) moment in the public ministry of Jesus Christ: his raising of Lazarus from the dead. This miraculous work (which is unique to John's gospel) is accompanied by yet another of the "I am" statements that Jesus has been making throughout the book—this one presenting him as humanity's ultimate hope for resurrection unto eternal life. Jesus brings Lazarus back to life—although he will face death a second time—as a foretaste of the great final resurrection yet to come.

John introduces us to Lazarus at the beginning of the chapter and tells us that he is ill, and Mary and Martha, his sisters, send urgent word to Jesus (11:1–3). Jesus immediately identifies the purpose that God has ordained for Lazarus's illness—and he chooses to stay where he is for two more days before making the trip to Lazarus's home in Judea (11:4–6). On the way, his disciples again struggle to understand his explanation of the actions he is taking in the wake of Lazarus's death (11:7–16). When Martha hears that Jesus is approaching, she goes out to meet him and speaks of the belief that she has in his power (11:17–22). Jesus responds to what she says by describing himself as the "resurrection and the life" and says that those who believe in him have life everlasting (11:23–26). Martha then expresses her faith that Jesus is the "Son of God" (11:27).

Prompted by an ensuing encounter that he has with Mary and by the grief around him, Jesus then displays deep emotion (11:28–37). Yet he steps forward, gives instructions for the stone to be rolled away from the tomb, and commands Lazarus to come out (11:38–44). While this miracle leads many to believe in him (11:45), the chief priests and the Pharisees feel threatened by his popularity and power (11:46–48). With the guidance of Caiaphas, the high priest, they begin to make plans to kill him (11:49–53). The chapter concludes as Jesus retreats to the wilderness and the Jews wonder whether he will dare to show himself in public at the upcoming Passover Feast in Jerusalem (11:54–57).

Read John 11:1–57.

GETTING STARTED

1. Have you ever been to a funeral or memorial service for someone whose mourners demonstrated no hope but only grief and pain? Contrast this with any other services you have attended at which the people around you, as well as the service itself, expressed great hope. What made the difference?

2. How often do you think about death? Why is it perhaps good for Christians to intentionally and habitually consider death—as well as the hope we have of being resurrected and experiencing the new heaven and new earth? What keeps you from thinking about these future realities more consistently?

OBSERVING THE TEXT

3. What does this chapter demonstrate about Jesus's sovereign and intentional plan? What does he teach his disciples about the purposes that God the Father, and he himself, have for even intense human pain and suffering?

4. In what different ways do people respond to Jesus throughout this passage? What is deeply encouraging about some of them—and maddening about others?

5. What truths about himself does Jesus teach—and directly demonstrate—by miraculously raising Lazarus from the dead? What effect does studying this chapter have on your understanding of Jesus's identity and power?

Gospel of Belief, pg. 31

The Gospel of John is sometimes called the Gospel of Belief. And if there is one place above all where this Gospel most powerfully summons us to faith in Jesus Christ, it might be here. Can there be a greater reason to believe on Jesus than his claim to hold the key to the problem of death? Jesus promises life: abundant life, and eternal life.

UNDERSTANDING THE TEXT

6. What do we learn about Jesus from the description of his relationship with Martha, Mary, and Lazarus in the opening verses of this chapter (11:1–6)? What does Jesus do after he hears the news about Lazarus's illness (v. 6)? What reasoning does he give for this course of action, and what does it teach us about his priorities?

7. What do the disciples struggle to understand, in 11:7–16, regarding Jesus's intentions behind what he is doing? How do they demonstrate the faith they still have in Jesus, and their willingness to follow him, even when they are confused?

8. What does Martha reveal about her view of Jesus through what she initially says to him (11:17–22)? What does he say to give sharper focus to her hope—and what does Martha do to immediately show that she understands and accepts his teaching (11:23–27)?

The Lord's Loving Timetable, pg. 11

Jesus' response to Lazarus's illness shows not only his perspective on our trials, but also *his plan* for delivering us from trouble. . . . The Lord works in our lives according to his timetable and his purposes. He is loving enough not to do what we want him to do but what we need him to do.

9. What do we learn from 11:28–37 about the heart Jesus has for sufferers? What do the actions he takes and the emotions he displays in this section tell us about him? What encouragement can these verses offer us when we ourselves are suffering?

10. What does Jesus do, in 11:38–44, to demonstrate boldly and authoritatively the power he has over death? What details in these verses make it clear to John's readers that Lazarus was truly, physically dead—and thus that this is a true and miraculous resurrection?

11. While many of the Jews go on to believe in Jesus after this miracle (11:45), it also prompts the Jewish leaders to coordinate their plots against his life even more intentionally (11:46–53). What does this remind us about the different responses we should expect to receive when we speak of Jesus, the gospel, and the resurrection? What questions are readers of John's gospel left with as the chapter concludes (11:54–57)?

A Voice That Wakes the Dead, pg. 59

Jesus cried, "Lazarus, come out" (John 11:43), and the man who was dead came back to life. This is the Savior that we need, the saving Lord whom we must trust. He is the Savior whose power conquered death by his resurrection. And on that great day to come, when Christ cries out once more, it will be the voice of our loving Savior that we hear.

BIBLE CONNECTIONS

12. Read Psalm 16:9–11. What relation do you see between the events of John 11 and these verses? What ultimate hope must David have in view, given his own eventual death and bodily decay; and how does the conversation that Jesus has with Martha point to this hope as well?

13. Read 1 Corinthians 15:35–49. How do we know that the resurrection Paul is describing in those verses is different from the one that Lazarus experiences in our passage from John?

THEOLOGY CONNECTIONS

14. Question 1 of the Westminster Shorter Catechism—"What is the chief end of man?"—is answered in this way: "Man's chief end is to glorify God and to enjoy him forever." What does our passage say that Jesus's "chief end" is, and what actions does it lead him to take? What impact do these actions have on the people around him—and what does this teach us about the difficulties involved in pursuing our chief end?

15. While John 11 demonstrates Jesus's full divinity by showing the authority he has over life and death, it also reveals his full humanity. Jesus is God—he raises a dead man to life. Jesus is a man—he weeps with compassion as he witnesses the grief and pain of those he loves. Why is it important for us to cling to both the full divinity and full humanity of Jesus Christ? What do we lose when we emphasize one of these to the exclusion of the other?

APPLYING THE TEXT

16. How should this passage impact the way that we think about God's hidden and sovereign purposes, even when we're experiencing pain, grief, and suffering? How should we act regarding the will of our God—even when we don't understand it?

17. What are some things you observe about Jesus in this passage that serve to increase your confidence in the prayers that you offer—and why?

18. What does this passage cause you to feel about the resurrection to come? How does it affect your thoughts and feelings about death—either your own death or that of faithful believers you know?

PRAYER PROMPT

As you close your study of this passage with prayer today, praise God for the hope of resurrection that we have through Jesus—the "resurrection and the life"! Ask him for the faith to believe in Jesus and to cling to him through pain, grief, suffering, and even death. Pray for a humble heart so that you can accept God's sovereign purposes, even when you do not understand them, because you know that he works for his sovereign glory—and our good—in all things.

LESSON 2

COSTLY WORSHIP AND ANGRY REJECTION

John 12:1–50

THE BIG PICTURE

The chapter you will study for this lesson is filled with starkly contrasting responses to Jesus the Messiah. From worshipful devotion to murderous plots, and from adoring shouts to embarrassed silence, John demonstrates the saving belief of some . . . and the stubborn rejection of others. As Jesus moves toward his climactic confrontation with the Jewish leaders in Jerusalem, John again presents the readers of his gospel with an invitation to *believe* that this Jesus is the Son of God and to find *life* in his name!

John 12 begins with the beautiful account of Mary's anointing of Jesus at Bethany (12:1–8), during which she pours out expensive ointment in a worshipful expression of devotion to Jesus—though Judas Iscariot objects to this (v. 6). After mentioning the plot that is brewing to kill Lazarus (12:9–11), John describes the entrance Jesus makes into Jerusalem as the Passover Feast draws near—the event that is often referred to as the "triumphal entry" (12:12–19). Even as the Pharisees continue to grumble angrily at Jesus's popularity, the crowds cry out in worship and celebration (v. 13).

When some gentile Greeks seek Jesus out, he foretells his death along with the fact that it will "draw all people" to himself (12:20–35). Yet many of the people, though they are fascinated by him, still do not believe in him—despite his call for them to do so (12:36–43). John applies Isaiah's prophecy about blindness and hardness of heart to the Jewish leaders who are rejecting Jesus, and he notes that they are after earthly "glory" rather than the "glory that comes from God" (v. 43).

The chapter concludes as Jesus speaks on behalf of the Father who has sent him, inviting all to believe in him in order to find life and light (12:44–50).

Read John 12:1–50.

GETTING STARTED

1. Have you ever known someone who was interested in Jesus but never devoted his or her life to him in worship, obedience, and faith? Why do you think this is the case for some people? What causes this kind of response to Jesus to fall far short of what he asks?

2. What made Jesus's sacrificial death central to the purpose behind his coming to earth? What does Jesus become if we leave out his death on the cross?

OBSERVING THE TEXT

3. Describe some of the different responses that you see people having to Jesus in John 12. Which responses would you say are the most extreme (both positively and negatively)?

4. Jesus offers several invitations to his hearers throughout this passage. What response does he call people to make to him, his teaching, and his ministering among them?

5. In this chapter, Jesus speaks explicitly several times about his death. What does he say to indicate that the crucifixion will be the central work he will perform as the Messiah?

UNDERSTANDING THE TEXT

6. What does this passage suggest is Mary's motivation for anointing Jesus (12:1–3)? What does Judas claim is the reason he is objecting to this act of worship (12:4–5)? What are his true motivations—and what do they foreshadow (12:6–8)?

Devotion Poured Out, pg. 79

The devotion for Jesus that was modeled by Mary, challenged by Judas, and threatened by the corrupt leaders was richly rewarded by the Lord. . . . There can be no greater reward than to be used in this way to share the glory of Christ in the world, knowing that as we pour out our devotion to him, he will pour out through us the grace of his gospel for the salvation of those we know and love.

7. Why are the chief priests planning to kill Lazarus, as well as Jesus, according to 12:9–11? What does this suggest about the expectations that followers of Jesus should have?

8. What does John present Jesus's "triumphal entry" into Jerusalem as being (12:12–19)? What do the people affirm and celebrate about Jesus? What hint does John give regarding the fickle nature of the crowd (v. 18)—and how do the Pharisees react to this dramatic scene (v. 19)?

9. What is Jesus's response when he hears that some Greeks are seeking him (12:20–26)? What encouragement can this offer to all gentiles who seek Jesus and want to be his disciples?

10. How does Jesus describe the chief motivation and calling that he has while he is in the world, and what does God do to affirm him (12:27–29)? What does Jesus say about his coming death as he invites his listeners, again, to believe in him (12:30–36)?

11. John notes that many people still refuse to believe in Jesus, despite all the signs he has performed (12:36–43). What prophesies are their responses to him fulfilling? What warning does Jesus give to those who reject him (12:44–50)?

BIBLE CONNECTIONS

12. Isaiah 53:1 is quoted in John 12:38. Read all of Isaiah 53:1–5 for the context of that verse. What do these verses tell us about the Suffering Servant—and specifically about the sacrificial death he will die for God's people?

13. John indicates that Jesus's triumphal entry into Jerusalem is a fulfillment of the prophecy of Zechariah; read Zechariah 9:9–13 now. What does the prophet say that this coming king will accomplish for God's people?

The King Will Come Again, pgs. 89–90
Jesus is not finished. When he returns in the glory of his kingdom, when all who reject him are judged and all sin is put away in hell, then Jesus will look upon a whole world that he has saved. For the King is coming again, and the book of Revelation depicts him then as riding not a donkey but a horse for war.

THEOLOGY CONNECTIONS

14. The Westminster Confession of Faith explains that "the principal acts of saving faith are accepting, receiving, and resting upon Christ alone for justification, sanctification, and eternal life, by virtue of the covenant of grace" (14.2). Where in John 12 do you see evidence of true saving faith that is occurring, and what distinguishes it from mere fascination with Jesus?

15. John 12 shows us that some people can sing loud praises to Jesus (v. 13) while not fully believing in him (vv. 37–40). What can we learn from this about true conversion? What marks of true faith should we look for in ourselves—and in all those who profess to have faith in Jesus Christ?

The Reality of Jesus, pg. 124

[Jesus] was sent by God, he revealed God, and he brought light to the world. If you have not believed, will you not face the reality of who and what Jesus is? If you have believed, then these are reasons why you must press on in faith, despite whatever difficulties you experience in this world.

APPLYING THE TEXT

16. Mary's anointing of Jesus demonstrates worship and devotion that is not only faith filled but costly. What might it cost you to follow Jesus in your current season or situation—and are you prepared to embrace that cost? How can you better prepare for this?

17. What does John 12 teach us about the fickle nature of the crowds we are all often tempted to follow? How can we cultivate the steady, consistent faith and obedience that Jesus's disciples should have?

18. How can you tell whether you have become a "[son] of light" through your belief in Jesus (12:36)? How can this passage help you to evaluate your own faith, obedience, and discipleship?

PRAYER PROMPT

As you close your study of John 12, consider the many contrasting ways you have seen people reacting to Jesus in this passage. Pray for God to grant you a humble belief in Jesus as the Son of God and the Savior of sinners, who was ultimately "lifted up" for your salvation (12:32). Ask him to give you faith in Jesus that will help you to serve him. In acknowledgment of the fact that he is the one who has the authority of God the Father, ask God to help you to obey him and offer him your costly devotion.

LESSON 3

SERVANT SAVIOR

John 13:1–38

THE BIG PICTURE

Many biblical scholars agree that John 13:1 marks the start of the second half of John's gospel, in which the narrative slows down significantly in order to spotlight Jesus's actions and words in the final hours before his betrayal and death. As this verse indicates, Jesus will love his disciples "to the end"—all the way to the cross, where he will lay down his life in their place.

As John's account slows its pace, we find Jesus with his disciples during the Feast of the Passover (v. 1). Jesus surprises the others by wrapping himself with a towel and stooping to wash their feet—a shocking expression of servanthood and humility (13:2–11). He then calls the disciples to serve one another humbly as a part of following their Master and Lord (13:12–20). After this, Jesus speaks of the imminent betrayal that is coming from one of his own disciples (13:21–30). Since he does not name his betrayer, the disciples ask who he might mean. Satan then enters into Judas Iscariot, who leaves abruptly and goes out under the cover of night.

As the chapter concludes, Jesus offers a "new commandment" to his disciples: they are to "love one another" (13:31–35). He notes that their love for one another should mark them to such an extent that, by it, the world will realize that they are his disciples. Then, when Peter declares his loyalty to him, Jesus predicts that Peter will deny him (13:36–38).

So we see how the servant Savior will go to the cross: betrayed by a close follower, denied by a friend, and yet determined to remain obedient to the will of the Father for the sake of the salvation of God's people. Jesus will love, serve, lead, and even die for his fickle and sinful children—in order to make them his own forever.

Read John 13:1–38.

GETTING STARTED

1. Why is it so difficult for us to serve others? What sinful attitudes and mindsets tend to emerge at moments when we're called to do something that requires humility—or that makes us feel small or insignificant?

2. In what contexts do you find it most difficult to stand boldly for Jesus, God's Word, and the gospel? Why is that?

OBSERVING THE TEXT

3. What about John 13:1 suggests that a new section of John's gospel has begun? What does this verse indicate will be the theme of this section?

4. What does Jesus call his disciples to do throughout this passage? In particular, what examples does he call them to imitate?

5. What role does Satan seem to play in Judas's betrayal of Jesus? What do we learn about Jesus from the way he treats Judas in this chapter?

UNDERSTANDING THE TEXT

6. Before John describes Jesus's act of washing his disciples' feet, what important context does he provide for it (13:1–3)? What fuels this humble service that Jesus performs (v. 3)?

Love to the End, pg. 139

Jesus loved his own to the end of his own life. Undoubtedly, this was John's major point of view, since this passage takes place in the shadow of the cross. If love for his own required Jesus to die for their sins, then he loved them to that end; the cross was indeed the fullest extent of his love.

7. Why are Jesus's disciples so shocked when he washes their feet (13:4–11)? What does Peter say as he is doing this—and what is Jesus's response to him? What does he say that the footwashing symbolizes?

8. What explanation does Jesus give his disciples for the humble act of service he performs by washing their feet (13:12–20)? What is he calling them to do for one another—and how are their attitudes and actions to be impacted, going forward, by this interaction?

9. Under whose control is Judas—and what hint of this did we get in 13:2? And yet what indications does John give us in 13:21–30 that all the events that are taking place lie within Jesus's sovereign plan, control, and foreknowledge?

10. What does 13:31–35 say ought to characterize Jesus's disciples in the eyes of the world? What is to be the basis of the disciples' love for one another—and what is the ultimate example of such love?

11. What evidence do you see that Peter is thinking too highly of himself and asserting his loyalty too boldly (13:36–38)? What sobering prediction does Jesus make regarding Peter, and what warning can this offer to all those who are too confident in their own strength and courage?

BIBLE CONNECTIONS

12. Read Philippians 2:1–11. How does Paul tie *our* attitude and mindset to the attitude and mindset of Jesus Christ? What hope lies ahead for Jesus—and for all who follow him?

13. Hebrews 6:4–6 discusses those who have "tasted" in some way of the goodness of God in the context of the community of faith . . . only to fall away and reject him. How does this description match what we have seen of Judas?

Fellowship and Betrayal, pg. 165
The danger [when we are betrayed] is that we might turn to bitterness and malice, but Jesus did not do that with Judas. Yet it is clear that our Lord suffered emotionally at the betrayal. . . . Therefore, when we are abandoned by loved ones or betrayed because of our Christian convictions, we may take solace in the fellowship we have with our Lord, who was even more wickedly betrayed.

THEOLOGY CONNECTIONS

14. Why is it important for us to understand that we have been *saved* by Christ's work before we see it as an *example* for us to follow? What dangers do we face, though, if we never consider that Jesus has set for us an example of humility, sacrifice, and service?

15. That Judas would betray Jesus is sobering—and it raises many theological questions. How could a man follow Jesus so closely for over three years . . . and then turn and betray the Son of God? Was Judas "saved," only to fall away—or had he never truly believed? Look back at John 12:4–6. What hint might John have been giving us, in those verses, that Judas's heart never fully belonged to Jesus? Even before he betrayed Jesus and took part in his death, what idol seems to have ruled in Judas's heart?

We Must Wash the Feet of Others, pg. 146
It will be when the world sees us ministering with humble, tender love to the stinky feet of each other's lives—the places where there is pain, ugliness, failure, and need—that it will realize that the Spirit of God is in our midst. To do this, just as Jesus took off his garments, we must take off all our pride, all our envy, and everything else that hinders us from taking up the basin to wash the feet of others.

APPLYING THE TEXT

16. Jesus is our Savior—but he teaches his disciples that he is also our example. Why is following Jesus's example unavoidable for those who truly know him and love him?

17. Think of those whom you know in the body of Christ and the needs that they have. What acts of humble service are you perhaps being called to perform for them right now? In what ways, if any, would you say that your love for God's people has marked you as a follower of Christ and thus served as a striking witness to the people around you?

18. What warning should you take from Judas's betrayal of Jesus—as well as from Peter's overconfident assertion about his own loyalty? What can these examples teach us about our own weakness, sin, and need for God's strength and grace?

PRAYER PROMPT

As you close your study of this remarkable chapter, ask God to give you a humble heart like that of your humble Savior, whose ultimate act of service to you was dying on the cross so that you would have eternal life. Pray for the ability to be willing to serve and love God's people joyfully, the way Jesus has served and loved you. And ask God for humility that will allow you to refuse to trust in your own strength and willpower in order to keep you faithful to him—but will rather lead you to rely on his strength, his support, and his Spirit.

LESSON 4

THE WAY

John 14:1-31

THE BIG PICTURE

John 14 is full of rich and gracious promises. As the troubled disciples ask Jesus questions about the departure he has foretold, he comforts them with words of hope—not only for the eleven of them but for all who will believe in him.

After Jesus tells his disciples that he is going to prepare a place for them with his Father, Thomas speaks up first and asks him how they can know the way there (14:1-5). Jesus answers by saying that he *himself* is the way—and the truth and the life (14:6-7). Then Philip asks Jesus to reveal the Father more fully to them (14:8). Jesus's response again links himself, his ministry, and his witness with God the Father: he assures the disciples that if they have seen and believed in him, they have truly come to know the Father (14:9-14).

Jesus next focuses on a wonderful gift that will follow his departure: the powerful presence and help of God the Holy Spirit (14:15-31). The disciples will receive this "Helper" from the Father at Jesus's request (vv. 15-17). If they live obediently, Jesus assures them, they will experience full fellowship with the three-person God: the Father, Son, and Holy Spirit (vv. 18-24). The coming Holy Spirit will be a "Helper" for Jesus's disciples, by teaching them the truth, giving them peace, and reminding them of all that Jesus has taught them, so that they can faithfully bear witness to the gospel even when they endure times of trouble and persecution (vv. 25-31).

Read John 14:1–31.

GETTING STARTED

1. Where do you tend to turn first when you face discouragement, weariness, fear, or anxiety? What tempts you to turn to sources of comfort other than the promises God has made you in Christ?

2. How and when do you tend to think about the Holy Spirit? What roles do you understand him to be playing in your daily life?

OBSERVING THE TEXT

3. What do the disciples say throughout this passage to reveal their lack of understanding, their anxiety, and even their fear? In what ways can we perhaps see ourselves in their struggle and uncertainty?

A Matchless Gift, pg. 280

Christ gives us peace so that we may rise and go to the world, unfazed by its scorn and undaunted by Satan's opposition, so that others might know the glory of God, who is great above all, believe in the gospel of Christ, and receive through faith his matchless gift of peace.

4. What specific promises and words of hope does Jesus offer to his disciples throughout this chapter? To whom does he point those whose hearts are troubled and fearful (14:1)?

5. How does Jesus, in the second half of this passage, describe the role that belongs to God the Holy Spirit? Is this the way you normally think about his role? Why, or why not?

UNDERSTANDING THE TEXT

6. What attitude and mindset within the disciples does Jesus address as this chapter opens (14:1)? What hope and encouragement should people whose hearts are troubled derive from what he says, and promises, in verses 1 through 4?

A Place for His Own, pg. 199

How wonderful it is to find a room prepared after a long journey. All who believe and trust in Christ can know that heaven has been prepared for their arrival. Our Mediator and Savior has carried our names into heaven and made a reservation there for us. No Christian will ever appear in heaven either unknown or unexpected, for Jesus has prepared a place there for each and every one of his own.

7. What does Thomas seem to be confused about in verse 5? What answer does Jesus give to his question—and what makes this answer consistent with the calls and invitations we have seen him issuing throughout the gospel of John up to now (14:6–7)?

8. What request does Philip make to Jesus in 14:8? What does Jesus then explain, again, about his relationship with God the Father (14:9–12)? What does he say this relationship means regarding his own authority—and the power he has to provide for those who believe in him (14:13–14)?

9. What does Jesus promise in 14:15–17? What relationship will the Spirit have with his disciples? Who will have an active role in the giving of the Spirit—and how?

10. What does 14:18–24 say are signs of genuine love for Jesus? What does Jesus say about the relationship that people who believe God's Word and obey his commands enjoy with him?

11. What additional roles does Jesus say the Holy Spirit will play in the lives of his disciples (14:25–26)? What promise does Jesus make to them in 14:27? What lies ahead for the disciples, and what does Jesus do to prepare them for what is coming (14:28–31)?

BIBLE CONNECTIONS

12. Read 2 Peter 3:8–10, which speaks of the final upheaval that will befall the created order when Jesus returns to judge the world. What hope does this passage offer us?

13. Near the opening of Acts, Luke mentions the command Jesus gives his disciples to "wait" in Jerusalem before he promises them that the Holy Spirit will come. Read Acts 1:1–5. What does Jesus indicate about the coming of the Holy Spirit?

THEOLOGY CONNECTIONS

14. Jesus's famous declaration of being "the way, the truth, and the life" reveals a core doctrine of the Christian faith: the *exclusivity of Christ*. This doctrine teaches that Jesus is the *exclusive* way to salvation—that there is no other way for sinful people to be redeemed. What makes this doctrine so important? How can it be said that the salvation Jesus offers is wonderfully *inclusive* as well?

15. Answer 6 of the Westminster Shorter Catechism tells us that "there are three persons in the Godhead; the Father, the Son, and the Holy Ghost; and these three are one God, the same in substance, equal in power and glory." In what way does John 14 make the doctrine of the Trinity clear, and what distinct roles does it depict the persons of the Godhead playing?

Comfort and Encouragement, pg. 259

Jesus' teaching was designed to comfort his disciples with the knowledge of his continuing work in them by the Holy Spirit. We should thus be greatly encouraged by the power of Christ available to us through the Spirit, who comes alongside us and calls within us so that we can achieve our potential as born-again citizens of the kingdom of Christ.

APPLYING THE TEXT

16. Jesus tells his disciples twice in John 14 not to let their hearts be "troubled" (vv. 1, 27). What specific promises that he makes in this passage should we cling to when our hearts are troubled, anxious, or afraid?

17. How should your understanding of the ministry that God the Holy Spirit works and the role he plays in your life be shaped and expanded by what you've read in this passage? Why should you be grateful for the presence of the Holy Spirit, who has been sent by God the Father and God the Son to indwell all believers?

18. What practical steps could you take to pursue peace rather than anxiety, and hope rather than fear, as Jesus taught his disciples to do in this passage? How could other people of God help to remind you of the invitation Jesus has given you to live in his peace and hope?

PRAYER PROMPT

As you close your study of John 14, praise God for the words of comfort it shows Jesus offering to his disciples—and therefore to *you*, if you have put your faith in him! Thank God, your Father, for the home that you have in heaven. Praise him for the gift of the Holy Spirit, who indwells you, comforts you, teaches you, and offers you God's peace along the way.

LESSON 5

THE TRUE VINE

John 15:1–16:4

THE BIG PICTURE

John is continuing to record Jesus's final discourse in our passage for this lesson, which begins with an extended metaphor from Jesus about a vine and its branches (15:1–11). Jesus himself, as Lord and Savior, is the vine; and his disciples are the branches—their lives, vitality, obedience, and goodness flow from the only life-giving source that is perfectly pleasing to God: Jesus Christ himself. Unless they have faith in Jesus, all who seek to follow God are helpless, hopeless, and spiritually ineffective. Jesus then exhorts his disciples to love one another with the same kind of self-sacrificial love that he has for them, which will soon be fully revealed through his death on the cross (15:12–17).

Changing topics, Jesus then warns his disciples that since the world hates him (as will soon be fully revealed), they should expect it to hate them as well (15:18–25). After he speaks of the hope that the coming of the Holy Spirit will bring (15:26–27), when he will "bear witness" about Jesus and equip the disciples to bear witness as well, Jesus once more discusses the impending opposition that his followers should expect (16:1–4). As the passage closes, we see that all throughout this final discourse Jesus is continuing to seek to strengthen his disciples with beautiful words of encouragement and exhortation.

Read John 15:1–16:4.

47

GETTING STARTED

1. Have you struggled with the fact that some people who do *not* believe in Jesus still seem to be kind, pleasant, and generous? What questions has this caused you to wrestle with—and why?

2. Why is it so difficult for us to endure being disliked? Why do we long to be accepted and approved by those around us? What causes this longing to sometimes lead us to spiritual cowardice and sinful compromise?

OBSERVING THE TEXT

3. What does Jesus's word picture in the opening verses of John 15 help us to understand? Why do you think he uses this particular metaphor?

The True Vine and the Good Fruit, pg. 282

It was in comparison to Israel's failure that Jesus declared himself the "true vine." Israel became a false and wild vine through idolatry and wickedness. In contrast, how pleasing was the life of Jesus to God the Father! . . . The fruit that God desired from Israel but did not find, he gained for himself by sending his own Son to be the true vine, from which his new and righteous people would live and bear good fruit.

4. Where do you see the theme of fruit turning up in this passage? What would you say Jesus is using the word *fruit* to mean here?

5. In this passage, what specific encouragement does Jesus offer to the disciples as he advises them to anticipate hardship . . . and even hatred?

UNDERSTANDING THE TEXT

6. What metaphor does Jesus use to describe himself—and what roles does God the Father play within that metaphor (15:1–2)? How does the metaphor describe Jesus's disciples and the necessity of their relationship with him (15:1–5)? What are the spiritual implications of this metaphor for us?

7. What instructions does Jesus then give to his disciples (15:5–11)? What warnings accompany these instructions?

8. How does Jesus explain the genuine love with which he commands his disciples to "love one another" (15:12–13)? What role does 15:14–17 say that he played in the disciples' lives?

9. What kind of attitudes and reactions does Jesus tell his disciples to expect the world to have regarding them (15:18–25)? What is his explanation for why this kind of treatment and hatred makes sense? And while these predictions were likely sobering, what encouragement might they have also provided to Jesus's disciples?

10. Jesus describes the coming of the Holy Spirit in 15:26–27. What role does he say the Holy Spirit will play, in the world and in relation to the disciples' actions and words?

Sacrifice and Suffering, pg. 312

According to Jesus . . . an easy, persecution-free Christianity is far from normal. Indeed, a kind of Christian faith that involves no sacrifice and produces no opposition from the world is, according to the New Testament, not true Christianity at all. Paul stated plainly: "All who desire to lead a godly life in Christ Jesus will be persecuted" (2 Tim. 3:12).

11. What kind of suffering does Jesus tell his disciples to anticipate—and what does he say is the reason he is telling them about all this before-hand (16:1–4)? In what way do these verses demonstrate his loving concern for his disciples (and for their faithfulness and endurance)?

BIBLE CONNECTIONS

12. Read Isaiah 27:1–6. How do these prophetic verses expand your under-standing of the meaning of what Jesus says in John 15:1–11? Why do you think he chose this picture to describe his disciples' relationship to him?

13. Look at Acts 5:40–41. What is the apostles' response to the treatment they receive in these verses? In what way do you think Jesus's words in John 15 may have prepared them to be able to have this reaction to suffering for him?

THEOLOGY CONNECTIONS

14. Jesus's insistence on the fact that the branches *must* abide in the vine in order to bear good fruit is a striking example of the doctrine of *total depravity*. This doctrine reminds us that, apart from the regenerating work of the Holy Spirit, we cannot choose God and live for him, because we are spiritually dead and utterly fallen. How can this vine-and-branches metaphor that Jesus uses help you to understand the reality of sin, and the miracle of salvation, more clearly?

15. In 1536, William Tyndale was strangled to death and then burned as a condemned "heretic." His crime? Translating the Scriptures into English. From what we have seen in John 15, what would you say was the deeper motivation behind his execution? In what way should we react to the example of martyrs such as Tyndale—and why?

Perfect Divine Joy, pg. 300

Do you find that you long for the fullness of Christ's joy in your life? . . . We do not need to live joyless lives, but we do need to abide in Christ, relishing his love, offering our obedience in return, and then abounding in the perfect divine joy that he has eternally possessed and that he delights to give to those who abide in him.

APPLYING THE TEXT

16. How can you tell if you are abiding in Jesus rather than seeking to live by your own strength, wisdom, and effort? What are some diagnostic questions or tools that might be able to help you to determine if you, as a branch, are truly abiding in Jesus, the vine?

17. What can you learn from this passage about what self-sacrificial love for your brothers and sisters in Christ is like? If Jesus laid down his life for you, what implications does that have regarding what you should do with your own preferences and interests for the sake of your fellow believers?

18. What encouragement should disciples of Jesus Christ feel when they are hated because of their faithfulness to the gospel? What truths is it important for us to remember when we experience rejection, mockery, or social marginalization specifically because of our commitment to Jesus Christ and the Word of God?

PRAYER PROMPT

As you close your study of this passage, ask God the Father for the Spirit to give you the strength to *abide* in Jesus Christ, the life-giving vine. Pray to be able to more deeply understand and accept the utter dependence you have on your Savior—not only for your sins to be forgiven but also for your life to be able to be fruitful and obedient. Ask God for patience and faithfulness and for the willingness to be hated and despised for the sake of Jesus, your Savior.

LESSON 6

A GOOD DEPARTURE

John 16:4–33

THE BIG PICTURE

In the passage for this lesson, Jesus continues to prepare his disciples to live, obey, and witness faithfully after his crucifixion, resurrection, and ascension. He is realistic about the suffering they will experience in his name—and yet his assurance is clear: all who follow him serve the glorious Savior who has "overcome the world" (16:33).

Speaking again of the Holy Spirit, Jesus now reveals that it will be *better* for him to go away, and for the Helper to come, than it would be for Jesus to remain physically present in the world (16:4–11). The reason it will be to the disciples' "advantage" for the Holy Spirit to come is because he will bring conviction to the world, through their witness, about the realities of sin, righteousness, and judgment (vv. 9–11). The Spirit will also play a guiding role in the lives and witness of his disciples by leading them to the truth about Jesus and glorifying him in the process (16:12–15).

When the disciples express confusion and sorrow over this, Jesus offers them another promise: their grief over his death and departure will ultimately turn to joy (16:16–24). Though his followers will mourn over his death (while the sinful world rejoices), their sorrow will not last. After Christ has risen and ascended, they—through the power of the Holy Spirit—will joyfully take part in the work of gospel witness as his redeemed people.

The chapter concludes as Jesus again affirms the authority and purpose that have been given to him (16:25–28). His disciples, who seem to reach a point of at least partial understanding, affirm their belief that Jesus has come "from God" (16:29–30). Then, despite predicting that they will abandon him soon after, Jesus offers the disciples a final word of affirmation and encouragement: they can have peace through him, even during tribulation, for he has overcome the world (16:31–33).

Read John 16:4–33.

GETTING STARTED

1. Has it ever happened that after you longed for something (and perhaps even prayed earnestly for it), God provided something even better than you had hoped for? How did that affect your view of God and your relationship with him?

2. What would you say is the main purpose of the Holy Spirit's activity on earth? In what other ways would people from different backgrounds or denominations perhaps answer that question?

Before the Cross, pg. 344

Jesus pointed out that there were truths that he had not taught the disciples because they were not yet ready or able to receive them. . . . This inability reflects not merely the disciples' weakness, but also the reality that they were still living before the cross. The pattern of God's revelation is for his saving action first to happen, and then for the biblical teaching to record and explain it.

OBSERVING THE TEXT

3. What is Jesus's argument for why his going away will actually be *better* for his disciples than if he stayed physically present with them on earth? What benefits will the coming of the Holy Spirit bring to them—and to the world?

4. What mindset do we see the disciples having as they consider Jesus's departure? What reference does Jesus make to their attitude and their feelings, in this passage, and what does he say in response to them?

5. How would you describe the perspective Jesus takes, in this chapter, regarding the difficulty of following him on earth? What transcendent hope does he say his disciples can have during suffering and hardship?

The Spirit's Application, pg. 335

This is why it is better for us that Jesus has departed for heaven: he has sent the Holy Spirit, who performs the work of conviction that is essential to any sinner's salvation. While on earth, Jesus *accomplished* our salvation, chiefly by dying for our sins. But now he has gone to heaven to send the Spirit, who *applies* what Jesus achieved to the individual soul through the gift of faith.

UNDERSTANDING THE TEXT

6. What does Jesus say, in 16:4–6, is causing the disciples' sorrow? What does Jesus tell the disciples he will do for them when he leaves (16:7)? What three kinds of "conviction" will the Holy Spirit bring to the world—and, as the disciples are preparing to bear witness about Jesus, what encouragement do you think this is offering them (16:8–11)?

7. What additional roles and actions does Jesus describe the Holy Spirit fulfilling in 16:12–15? What relationship will God the Holy Spirit have with God the Son and God the Father?

8. We see the disciples struggling to understand Jesus's predictions about what will happen in "a little while" in 16:16–19. What seems to be confusing to them—and what do you think is making Jesus's words difficult for them to understand?

9. What comparison does Jesus use to describe the disciples in 16:20–22, and why? What does he ultimately promise them? What does he instruct them to do in the meantime—and what additional promises does he make to them (16:23–24)?

10. How does the disciples' relationship with Jesus play into their relationship with—and knowledge of—God the Father (16:25–28)? What clarity does Jesus say they will experience in the days to come? What assurances does he give them?

11. After Jesus affirms his disciples' belief, he indicates that trouble is coming (16:29–33). What statement of encouragement and hope does Jesus conclude this chapter with—and what does he mean by it?

Take Heart! pg. 382
You may rely on [Christ's] victory when you feel yourself at the end and on the brink of failure. Our victory is Christ crucified for our sins and Christ living with power at God's right hand. Take heart! Christ has overcome the world!

BIBLE CONNECTIONS

12. Read Acts 2:37, which describes the effect that Peter's preaching about Jesus had on many of the unbelieving Jews in Jerusalem. How does this moment illustrate the teaching that Jesus relates in John 16:6–11?

13. Look at Romans 8:22–23, and notice how the apostle Paul describes the condition of all creation as it awaits the redemption it will experience upon Jesus's return. What imagery and language is he sharing from what Jesus says in John 16:21–22? What great hope does this fallen world—as well as God's redeemed, albeit "groaning," people—have?

THEOLOGY CONNECTIONS

14. The doctrine of *perspicuity* tells us that the most important truths about God, humanity, and salvation are clearly perceptible in God's Word. Yet what does John 16:13 tell us about the Holy Spirit's role? Why are Scripture and the Holy Spirit both essential participants in saving faith?

15. What does Jesus teach us about the work of the Holy Spirit in 16:14? What do the details of this verse indicate about what makes God the Holy Spirit's role distinct from those of God the Son and God the Father? And, with that being the case, why does praising and worshiping the Son also honor the work of the Spirit?

APPLYING THE TEXT

16. What does 16:12–15 show us we can do to honor the Holy Spirit and respond rightly to his work? How do these verses make it obvious that the Holy Spirit's agenda is not different from that of the Father and the Son? What connection do these verses say the Spirit's work will have with what Jesus has already accomplished and revealed?

17. Do you find it encouraging that Jesus has predicted the difficulty of following him in this world? Why or why not? What is the right way to think about persecution in light of the warnings—and the assurances—that Jesus includes in this passage?

18. What does this passage say, especially in verse 33, is our final and ultimate hope? Does the way you live your life reflect a confidence that great joy lies ahead of you? Why or why not?

PRAYER PROMPT

Begin your prayer, now that this lesson has ended, by thanking God that you follow a crucified, risen, and reigning Savior who has indeed overcome the world! As you seek to live by faith in Jesus Christ—to listen to his Word, believe in God the Father, and walk in obedience—thank God that he has sent the Holy Spirit to strengthen and equip you. Pray that, even when you are in the midst of sorrow, you will have the courage that comes from knowing that eternal joy lies ahead of you in Jesus, your Savior.

LESSON 7

THE HIGH PRIESTLY PRAYER

John 17:1–26

THE BIG PICTURE

As John 17 begins, Jesus transitions from warning, instructing, and encouraging his disciples to praying to the Father on their behalf. In this passage, we learn even more about Jesus's focus and priorities as his hour of glory approaches—and we discover that his prayer extends even to believers in the present day.

Jesus prays, first, about the glory the Father is going to bring to him through his death and resurrection (17:1–5). His death will have the purpose of granting "eternal life" to all who know God the Father through the Son. He prays specifically for his disciples—for those whom God the Father "gave [him] out of the world" (17:6)—and asks the Father to keep them in his name (17:7–15). He also prays for his disciples' sanctification—for them to be set apart by the Word for God's service (17:16–19).

As this prayer, which is often called Jesus's "High Priestly Prayer," comes to a close, he prays for all who will go on to "believe in [him] through [the disciples'] word"—that is, for all believers in the generations to come (17:20–26). He prays that they will be unified for the sake of the witness they will bear to the world about him. And as their unity reflects God the Father's unity with God the Son, Jesus asks for the love of God to dwell with and in his people, so that many others will come to believe in Jesus and receive salvation (v. 21).

Read John 17:1–26.

GETTING STARTED

1. Describe a time when a moment of crisis revealed someone's true priorities to you (even if they were your own!). Why can it be the case that the threat of death, or at least the upending of "life as usual," can lead someone to focus on the matters that are of utmost importance to them?

2. What is your response to hearing someone pray for you—especially if you are experiencing grief, pain, or some other difficulty? At what times have the prayers of God's people been particularly encouraging to you; and in what ways have you seen such prayers being answered?

OBSERVING THE TEXT

3. What do the opening verses of Jesus's prayer indicate about the main focus of his earthly life and ministry? Are you surprised by anything that Jesus prays about—or by anything that he does *not* include in this prayer?

4. What does Jesus reveal, in the middle section of this prayer, about the heart he has for his disciples? What priorities does he have for them? What does he want to occur in, and through, their lives and their witness?

5. What immediate *personal* application does this passage have for believers in Jesus today, and what comfort does it offer them (17:20–26)?

UNDERSTANDING THE TEXT

6. What would you say is the main theme of Jesus's prayer regarding himself in 17:1–5? What specific requests does he make of God the Father? What understanding does this prayer offer us of the way Jesus views his own work?

Priorities of the Heart, pg. 386

Jesus' concerns in the prayer of John 17 show us the priorities of his heart. First, Jesus prays not that the world would acclaim him but that God would approve and glorify him. Second, Jesus prays that the events to come would glorify the Father. Third, Jesus devotes most of his prayer to petitions for the salvation and blessing of his people. The crisis of Jesus' cross reveals his dying passion for the Father's glory and for the salvation of the elect who belong to him.

7. What does Jesus say his disciples have done in response to the work God the Father has performed in their lives (17:6–10)? What do these verses say that Jesus himself has done for the disciples, and what do they say his followers have done in response to the call of the Father and the teaching of Jesus?

8. What is the first big request that Jesus makes on behalf of his disciples in this prayer (17:11–14)? What does 17:15 say is threatening them?

9. What is the second big request that Jesus makes on behalf of his disciples (17:16–19)? Through what specific means does he anticipate that this request will be granted—and what does that teach us about the significance of Scripture?

The Glory of God's Love, pg. 411

It would especially be in his self-sacrifice of the cross that Jesus would display the Father to the world. He began his prayer by asking the Father to enable him to do this: "Father, the hour has come; glorify your Son that the Son may glorify you" (John 17:1). On the cross, Jesus displayed the glory of God's love and grace for sinners.

10. How would you summarize the request Jesus makes for those who will believe in him in the generations to come (17:20–23)? What effect will the granting of this request have on the world (vv. 21, 23), and why is that so important to Jesus?

11. What desire does Jesus have for his followers, and why should we derive deep encouragement and hope from this (17:24)? What work does 17:25–26 say that Jesus will continue to perform in the lives and hearts of those who believe in him?

BIBLE CONNECTIONS

12. Read Jude 24, which contains the words of assurance with which Jude begins his benediction to his readers. Which of the themes that we've seen within the prayer Jesus offers for his disciples is Jude perhaps referencing here? What makes the actions that God performs, which both Jude and Jesus pray about, a source of encouragement for redeemed sinners—and what hope should we take from them?

13. Look at 1 Corinthians 5:9–13. What connection is there between Paul's commands and Jesus's prayer for the unity and oneness of all who believe in him? What are the foundations of true Christian unity, and why does this unity sometimes require church discipline in order to be maintained?

THEOLOGY CONNECTIONS

14. Jesus prays specifically that God the Father would keep his disciples from the "evil one" (17:15). This verse, among others in Scripture, speaks to the reality of a personal devil—Satan—who not only exists but also seeks to harm God's people. Why is it important for us to remember this? What mistakes do we need to avoid regarding the way we think—or don't think—about Satan?

15. There are almost countless different denominations within the church today. At first it may seem that the church is thus failing to carry out Jesus's prayer about being unified—and yet what aspects of having different denominations are actually good and healthy? How, also, could Christians succeed at pursuing unity even when they are separated across different denominations?

APPLYING THE TEXT

16. What does Jesus's prayer tell you that you should hold as a priority? What specific impacts can you see this having on the way you live your life, engage in your relationships, and respond to the saving work he has done for you?

17. What encouragement should you take, and what strength should your faith experience, because of Jesus's prayer—specifically the part when he prays for protection for his disciples? What does this prayer reveal about the tender and loving heart that he has for his people?

18. What would it look like for you to pursue unity with other believers in the weeks and months ahead? With whom should you seek the kind of unity that Jesus prays for in this passage? Under what conditions might it be appropriate for you to break fellowship with someone—and with whom would this happen?

The Basis of Christian Unity, pg. 462
First, Christian unity requires us to believe what the Bible says. To remove obedience to Scripture does not promote but rather destroys true spiritual unity. Second, Christian unity requires us not to add to the Bible. Sadly, man-made rules and extrabiblical doctrines have often divided Christians who should be one.

PRAYER PROMPT

In this passage, you have heard Jesus praying for all his disciples—including you! Begin your own prayer by thanking God for the heart that your Savior has for you, and ask him to keep you in his name so that you don't stumble, turn away, or succumb to the attacks of Satan. Then ask him to graciously grant the Son's prayer for unity among believers—pray that you will be equipped to pursue peaceful, joyful, and godly relationships with other believers, for God's glory, in your church, community, and neighborhood.

LESSON 8

BETRAYED . . . YET IN CONTROL

John 18:1–27

THE BIG PICTURE

As John 18 opens, we find that Jesus's Farewell Discourse has ended—the time of his departure is now drawing near. This final section of John's gospel intentionally slows its pace as it describes the betrayal, arrest, abuse, crucifixion, and resurrection of Jesus Christ—the Son of God and the Savior of sinners, who will now be glorified as he is lifted high in the place of God's people. It is for their sake that he is suffering and dying—in order to bring them to eternal life when they believe in his name.

In the first part of the chapter, the soldiers and officers sent by the chief priests and the Pharisees arrest Jesus after Judas betrays him (18:1–11). Yet John indicates that Jesus is sovereignly in control throughout these events: the men who have come to bring him into custody fall down when he speaks, and Jesus himself is utterly calm—he even instructs Peter to put his sword away after Peter strikes the ear of the high priest's servant. Jesus clearly intends to go calmly to the cross—the place where he will accomplish his glorious work of salvation.

John juxtaposes Jesus's trial before Annas and Caiaphas with an account of Peter's denial of him (18:12–27). First, as he is warming himself while waiting in a courtyard, Peter denies being one of Jesus's disciples (vv. 15–18). The chief priests then question Jesus, and one of the soldiers strikes him (vv. 19–24). Meanwhile, when Peter is questioned by servants, he denies Jesus two more times (vv. 25–27). The passage concludes as a rooster crows, just as Jesus predicted.

Jesus, the Son of God, has been betrayed by Judas, denied by Peter, and unjustly tried by the Jewish religious leaders. And yet our Savior marches to the cross so that he can take our place and drink the "cup" the Father has given him.

Read John 18:1–27.

GETTING STARTED

1. Have you ever heard people tell the story of Jesus's betrayal and arrest as if he were a helpless, unwilling victim of injustice? What makes this a problematic way to understand what happened to him?

2. When you realize you have disobeyed or dishonored God, how do you react? What lies are you tempted to believe regarding the way God sees you when you fail?

OBSERVING THE TEXT

3. How does John demonstrate that Jesus remains *sovereign* over all the events that take place throughout this passage? What do you notice about how Jesus speaks during his arrest?

4. This passage gives strong evidence of the sinfulness and weakness of every human character other than Jesus Christ. Choose two or three characters from this passage and briefly describe their sin, failure, or weakness.

5. What hints does Jesus give in this passage about the meaning and purpose behind the death he will die on the cross? How can we tell that his disciples do not yet completely understand what he is saying?

UNDERSTANDING THE TEXT

6. What key figure returns to make an appearance in the opening verses of this chapter (18:1–6), and what actions does he take? How do these verses display the authority Jesus still has in the face of the band of soldiers who have come to arrest him?

Tragedy and Triumph, pg. 490

To be sure, the passion of Christ is the greatest of all tragedies. For those involved, these were the most dismal of days. . . . Yet, John insists, its message is a gospel of hope for those who love him, good news of a triumph that breaks out of the tragedy. Not only is the tragic cross followed by triumph, but the cross *is* the triumph.

7. What does Jesus do to demonstrate that, even while he is being arrested, he still cares for and protects his disciples (18:7–9)? What does the action that Peter takes in 18:10–11 demonstrate about his misunderstanding regarding Jesus's purpose? How does Jesus respond to this action?

8. Jesus is bound and led to the high priest to be questioned (18:12–14, 19–24). What does John remind us, in verse 14, that Caiaphas had said earlier about Jesus—and why do you think he does so?

9. While Jesus is before the high priest, John shifts the scene to Peter (18:15–18). What do you think leads Peter to respond to the servant girl's question in the way he does?

Christ's Sovereign Intentions, pgs. 497–98

The great point [of this passage], of course, is Christ's sovereignty in submitting to the Father's will for him to die on the cross. He would drink the cup of wrath so as to achieve our salvation. This is the true reason why Peter did not need his sword, since Jesus fully intended to be arrested.

10. In what way does Jesus choose to answer the high priest's questions (18:19–24)? Why does the officer in verse 22 strike Jesus? How does this "trial" ultimately conclude (v. 24)?

11. The narrative returns to Peter in 18:25–27. What does he do, twice, in quick succession? What do you think is his motivation for doing it? What do you think John wants to call our thoughts toward, in verse 27, when he mentions the detail about the rooster—and what would you say is his reason for doing this?

BIBLE CONNECTIONS

12. In John 18:11, Jesus speaks of the "cup" that the Father has given him to drink. Read Isaiah 51:17 and Zechariah 12:2. How do both of these prophetic passages help us to understand the significance, and the contents, of this "cup" to which Jesus refers?

Gospel Hope, pg. 509

Where . . . is the hope? The hope is found in realizing that Jesus walked his lonely road to the cross in order that he might be "wounded for our transgressions [and] . . . crushed for our iniquities" . . . (Isa. 53:5). This was Peter's own gospel hope, as expressed in his first epistle, a hope for all sinners who like the apostle so greatly need a Savior.

13. Look at Hebrews 7:25. In what way does it further develop the tender and constant care we see Jesus showing in John 18:9 to those who are entrusted to him by the Father? What more does Jesus do for believers beyond merely not *losing* them?

THEOLOGY CONNECTIONS

14. As we saw above, the "cup" that Jesus mentions is a reference to the wrath of God, which is poured out on sinners. This invokes the doctrine of *propitiation*—the teaching that Jesus fully satisfied God's wrath against sinners by bearing it in their place on the cross. What makes this such good news? What ought we to feel inspired to do because of this doctrine?

15. As Jesus draws nearer to the cross, he is not only opposed by the chief priests and betrayed by Judas but even denied by his closest disciple! What do you find significant about the fact that these final hours of Jesus's life illustrate the doctrine of *total depravity*, which teaches that every human being is fallen?

APPLYING THE TEXT

16. Why, and to what extent, ought we to see ourselves in Judas and Peter? In what way can this passage serve to strengthen our faith in the love and grace that Jesus has for us despite our sin?

17. What can we learn from the rash and violent way that Peter reacts to the injustice of the chief priests—as well as from the gracious correction that Jesus gives him?

18. What does Peter teach us about the opportunities and challenges that are involved in standing for Jesus in difficult—even dangerous—situations?

PRAYER PROMPT

John reveals the sovereign control that Jesus has, even when he is in his darkest moment, as well as the loving care he has for his disciples—the same disciples who are unfaithful to him and abandon him. Praise God for the faithful care he has for you as well, even though you have often failed him and denied him. Thank your faithful, sovereign Savior for marching toward the cross to save you—a helpless sinner.

LESSON 9

JESUS AND PILATE

John 18:28-19:16

THE BIG PICTURE

As we transition from the last lesson to this one, Jesus—now a prisoner—has changed hands, moving from his "trial" before the Jewish leaders to a confrontation with their Roman governor: Pontius Pilate. John allots much more time and space to the interaction between Jesus and Pilate than the other gospel writers do, in order to show us the clash between a powerful human ruler and the ruler of the universe—Jesus, the Son of God.

The passage begins as the Jewish leaders bring Jesus to Pilate and appeal to him to make a judgment against Jesus (18:28-32). Pilate initially wants nothing to do with what he views as a Jewish squabble, but the Jews make it clear that the punishment they have in mind for Jesus is death, which requires a ruling from Pilate (vv. 31-32). So he spends some time questioning Jesus in an effort to understand his claims and intentions (18:33-40). He struggles to understand the nature of Jesus's kingship, and Jesus explains that the kingdom he is building is not an earthly one (v. 36). After a cynical remark to Jesus about the nature of truth (v. 38), Pilate announces to the Jewish leaders that he finds no "guilt" in him and, in keeping with a practice that was common at the Passover, offers to release him (vv. 38-39). The Jews, in reply, clamor for Barabbas (who "was a robber") to be released instead of Jesus (v. 40).

Perhaps in an attempt to pacify the crowd, Pilate then flogs Jesus, who receives other forms of abuse and torture, as well, before Pilate brings him out again and announces the verdict that he is not guilty (19:1-6).

The Jews continue to push for Jesus's execution—now by bringing up the claim he has made that he is the Son of God (19:7–8). Now truly alarmed, Pilate begins his second round of questioning, but Jesus stops responding to him—except to deny that Pilate has ultimate authority over him (19:9–11). Even though his desire to release Jesus is growing, Pilate is ultimately overcome by the cries of the crowd, who warn him that no friend of Caesar would fail to judge Jesus and his claims (19:12–13). The Roman governor chooses self-preservation instead of submitting to Jesus and believing in him, and he gives him over to be crucified on his authority (19:14–16).

Read John 18:28–19:16.

GETTING STARTED

1. In what ways is your life affected by the fear of human authorities—whether they are political leaders, cultural influencers, or people in other positions of power? What aspects of ordinary life can tempt us to forget that God rules and has ultimate power over every human authority?

2. In what instances and situations have you given in to the influence of others rather than clinging to your convictions and obeying God's Word? Why is it so difficult for us to reject the voices of the crowd?

A Clash of Two Kingdoms, pg. 511
Little did Pilate appreciate that his meeting with Jesus involved a clash of two kingdoms, two value systems, and ultimately two judgments. While Pilate would decide Jesus' temporal fate, it was Pilate's eternal judgment that would be determined by his relationship to his prisoner, Jesus Christ.

OBSERVING THE TEXT

3. Throughout this passage, what are the Jewish leaders set on doing to Jesus? What seems to be their prevailing emotion, and what seems to be motivating them?

4. This passage vividly depicts the internal and external struggle Pilate undergoes as he seeks to determine what to do with Jesus—and how to respond to the angry crowd who are making their appeal to him. What competing forces and motivations play upon Pilate throughout this passage?

5. What does Jesus do throughout this passage to demonstrate that everything that is happening to him falls under the scope of his sovereignty and plan? What tone does he take as he answers Pilate, and what does he reveal about his ultimate purpose and identity?

Jesus Bore Our Shame, pg. 526
The Apostles' Creed lists the abuse of Jesus among the great redemptive events of his atoning work: "he suffered under Pontius Pilate." This physical abuse and public ridicule was part of what Jesus suffered for us in bearing our sins. . . . Not only was he "wounded for our transgressions" and "crushed for our iniquities" (Isa. 53:5), but he also bore the shame and reproach that our sins deserve.

UNDERSTANDING THE TEXT

6. What response does Pilate initially give to the Jews who bring Jesus before him (18:28–32)? What seems to be his motivation for giving this response? What authority does Pilate have, which the Jewish leaders lack (18:31)?

7. What is Pilate seeking to determine about Jesus during his initial interaction with him (18:33–40)? What does he say to reveal his spiritual skepticism and cynicism? In what way does he then try to appease the Jews—and how do they respond to his attempt?

8. What do you think is Pilate's motivation for having Jesus flogged and allowing him to be publicly ridiculed, mocked, and abused (19:1–4)? What would you say he is seeking to communicate to the Jews in 19:5?

A Friend of Jesus, pg. 540

Are you a friend of Jesus Christ, trusting in him, surrendering your will to him as your King and Lord? If you have renounced the friendship of Caesar and become a friend of Jesus, you can know that he died for your sins. He promises that whatever fire you endure in this world for his sake, he will go through it with you, so that you will not be consumed.

9. The back-and-forth that takes place between him and the Jews, in 19:6–9, seems to be a kind of turning point for Pilate. What change do his demeanor and attitude regarding Jesus go through afterward, and why?

10. When Jesus refuses to answer Pilate, in 19:9, what claim does Pilate use to threaten him—and why (19:10)? What response does Jesus make to this threat (19:11)? What does Pilate seek to do after this conversation (19:12)?

11. Despite the fact that he clearly understands that Jesus is not guilty, and desires to release him, Pilate ultimately gives the Jews permission to crucify him (19:16). What about their accusation in 19:12 might have driven Pilate to make this decision and forced the actions that he takes in 19:13? What final question does Pilate put to them before he turns Jesus over to be crucified (19:14–15)?

BIBLE CONNECTIONS

12. Read Isaiah 53:1–4. What fulfillment do these prophetic verses find in the brutal mistreatment Jesus undergoes in this passage? List specific words and phrases from this prophecy that are fulfilled here in John.

13. Look at Matthew 27:17–19. What additional detail does Matthew give us concerning Pilate's wife and what she tells her husband regarding Jesus? What does this do to compound Pilate's struggles?

THEOLOGY CONNECTIONS

14. Many churches regularly recite the Apostles' Creed—an ancient affirmation of Christian faith and belief that, among the other assertions it makes, says that Jesus "suffered under Pontius Pilate." Why do you think Pilate's name was included in this brief summation of Christian doctrine? What have Christians throughout the generations been called to remember about the clash of human and divine power that Jesus's trial represented?

15. The Westminster Larger Catechism says that the events in this passage are part of the way in which Jesus "humbled" himself, since, as answer 49 tells us, he willingly submitted to being "condemned by Pilate, and tormented by his persecutors." Why is it important for us to understand that Jesus has divine authority and power and, thus, that he willingly submitted to everything that happened to him in this passage? What does Jesus say, in the interaction he has with Pilate, to indicate this divine authority he holds?

APPLYING THE TEXT

16. Consider the various sinful reactions that you see people having to Jesus in this passage: hatred, rage, confusion, and skepticism. Have you, for the sake of Jesus, God's Word, and the gospel, experienced any of these reactions from people? What does Jesus teach you here about how to prepare for and respond to these things?

17. Pilate violated his own conscience by sending the Son of God to be crucified. What warning does this serve for everyone who faces pressure to deny or betray Jesus? What should we resolve to do, instead, when this happens?

18. What major risks does 19:12 indicate that Pilate would have taken if he had freed Jesus and denied the Jews' request? And we have already discussed the risks he did take, in areas such as his conscience, by delivering Jesus over to be crucified instead. How should we weigh the similar "risks" that are involved in our own lives, choices, and behavior?

PRAYER PROMPT

With this passage's showdown fresh in your mind, which took place between Jesus and Pilate as the shouts of the Jews echoed in the background, spend a few moments asking God for the courage, strength, and faith to be able to cling to Jesus and his kingdom—no matter the pressure, risk, or danger that this involves. Consider the abuse, shame, ridicule, and mockery that your Savior bore in your place, and ask him to help you to choose his eternal kingdom over all the pleasures and pressures of this world!

LESSON 10

THE CROSS OF CHRIST

John 19:16–42

THE BIG PICTURE

Jesus, after having been committed by the Roman governor to the Jewish leaders, now goes to the cross. In this great defining work—the work that he came to earth in order to accomplish—the Savior will die in the place of God's sinful people. Though he is despised by many, he will bring salvation to all who look to him in repentance and faith.

John's description of Jesus's crucifixion is sparse and matter of fact; he simply notes where it takes place and with whom Jesus is crucified (19:16–18). Interestingly, though, this sparse description gives us a glimpse into Pilate's internal struggle that the other gospels do not: he insists that the sign above Jesus read, "The King of the Jews"—much to the Jews' frustration (19:19–22). Thus Jesus's true identity is displayed as he dies for his sinful people.

Throughout his account of the crucifixion, John connects details regarding Jesus's death to prophecies from Scripture, so that "you"—the reader—might "believe" (v. 35). The soldiers' dividing of Jesus's garments, in 19:23–24, fulfills David's prophetic words from Psalm 22:18; and John links the thirst that he expresses in 19:28–29 to Psalm 69:21. When Jesus's side is pierced, John references the two prophecies from Scripture that this fulfills as well (19:31–37).

Jesus lovingly commits his mother, Mary, to John's care in 19:25–27. Then, before he dies, he utters one final declaration: "It is finished" (19:30)—

he has completed the work of salvation and fully drained the cup of God's wrath for the sake of his people.

His burial is then overseen by Joseph of Arimathea, a secret believer in Jesus, who is accompanied by Nicodemus, the Pharisee we met in John 3. Nicodemus's presence seems to indicate that he has responded to the words of life Jesus spoke to him with saving faith rather than taking part in his fellow Pharisees' murderous act against the Son of God (19:38–42).

Read John 19:16–42.

GETTING STARTED

1. In what ways have you heard people outside the church talk about Jesus's death on the cross? What meaning (if any) do they seem to attach to it?

2. Why do some people embrace Jesus's *teachings* but refuse to accept the necessity or the meaning of his *sacrificial death*? What does the fact that Jesus needed to die imply about the state of human beings and their standing before God?

Faithful, pg. 561

John labors to highlight Jesus' faithfulness. Jesus was faithful to God in fulfilling the prophecies of Scripture . . . so that God's saving plan might be fulfilled. Jesus was faithful to his mother, providing for her needs even while he suffered on the cross. Finally, Jesus was faithful to us as he bore our nakedness in sin, shed his crimson blood to cleanse us of our guilt, and provided the righteousness we need to stand in favor before God.

OBSERVING THE TEXT

3. What would you say are some of the main things John emphasizes as he recounts Jesus's crucifixion? What does he want you, the reader, to notice? What kind of information does he leave out that you might have wanted to know?

4. How many prophecies does John mention being fulfilled during this passage? Why do you think he sees their fulfillment as being so significant?

5. What indications does this passage give us about what Jesus's death means? Who seems to have saving faith in him? Which people continue to reject and disbelieve him?

Nothing Can Alter God's Will, pg. 550

God's will . . . truly [can] not be altered, and God's declaration of the righteousness, glory, and dominion of his Son can never be annulled by the indignant unbelief of rebel mankind. Thus was established the true cause of Jesus' death: He died because he was King of God's covenant nation and because only through his death could his beloved people be forgiven and enter eternal life.

UNDERSTANDING THE TEXT

6. What do you notice about the way John describes Jesus's crucifixion (19:16–18)? With whom is Jesus crucified?

7. Based on what we saw in our previous lesson, why do you think Pilate chooses the specific inscription that he puts on Jesus's cross in 19:19–22? Why do you think he is no longer so concerned about the Jews' opinions?

8. To what Old Testament prophecy does John link the soldiers' actions as they surround Jesus's cross (19:23–24)? What does Jesus reveal about his character during this time of excruciating and prolonged agony (19:25–27)?

9. What do both Jesus and John indicate to us about how Jesus understands the significance of his death, in the final two statements that John records him making (19:28–30)? What glorious good news do we find in his second statement: "It is finished"?

10. What do 19:31–37 say to make it clear that Jesus has truly, physically died? What further Scriptures are fulfilled through the fact that his side is pierced and his bones are not broken, and what do these things indicate about his death?

11. What do 19:38–42 tell us about Joseph of Arimathea? What other character reemerges within those verses—and is there anything surprising about his appearance? How do the actions of these two men compare to those we saw from Jesus's followers in the previous chapter?

BIBLE CONNECTIONS

12. There is perhaps no more vivid prophetic anticipation of the torments that Jesus experienced on the cross than Psalm 22. Read verses 1 through 18 of that psalm, and note several of the specific ways that the crucifixion fulfills David's prophecy.

13. Read Romans 3:21–26. What theological explanation does Paul give for everything that happens to Jesus on the cross? What does this passage help us to understand regarding what Jesus Christ's death means for sinners?

THEOLOGY CONNECTIONS

14. Many sermons, books, and even films have highlighted the *physical* agony that Jesus Christ went through on the cross, and it is true that this mode of Roman execution caused him immense and almost unimaginable physical agony. Yet we must remember that as the Son of God took on the weight of the sin of all God's people and bore the Father's wrath in their place, his greatest suffering was *spiritual*. What do we fail to appreciate if we focus *only* on the physical suffering that Jesus experienced?

Why Refuse to Call on Christ? pg. 551

Can you give any justifiable reason why you should not . . . hail Jesus as the true King of glory, the sinless Savior who died out of love for you, gaining your forgiveness by bearing the curse of your sins on the cross? If you refuse to call on Jesus for salvation, you will be joining the Jewish leaders in preferring to be damned forever rather than humble yourself in submission to Jesus and his cross.

15. While Jesus's final cry is brief, it is deeply theologically significant. We saw him speak earlier about the "cup" that the Father had given him to drink, which refers to an Old Testament picture of the *wrath* of God. With that in mind, what does his declaration here that his work is "finished" imply is true of sinners who hide themselves in Jesus by faith? What makes this wonderfully good news?

APPLYING THE TEXT

16. How do the Jewish leaders continue to illustrate their rebellion against God in this passage? What warning can this offer us about people who harden their hearts against Jesus, all the way to the end?

17. What signs do we see, in the conclusion of this passage, that Joseph and Nicodemus have faith in Jesus? What risks do they take, and how can their example serve to inspire us, as well, to have faith and courage as we follow Jesus today?

18. Read John 19:35 once more. What is the best way that you can respond to Jesus's death? What details within this passage most help you to respond in this way?

PRAYER PROMPT

Now that you have studied the climax of the gospel of John, take some time to meditate quietly on the significance of the death that the Son of God died for you—a sinner. Thank God for the way that the promises he made to his people throughout the generations were answered through the birth, life, and death of Jesus the Savior. Ask him to give you a humble, grateful, worshipful heart as you look upon the One who was pierced for your sins, in your place, and for your salvation.

LESSON 11

AN EMPTY TOMB

John 20:1–18

THE BIG PICTURE

We have seen that Jesus's death was no meaningless tragedy but was part of God's intentional and sovereign plan. By bearing God's wrath in the place of his sinful people, Jesus died to fulfill the promises God had made to reconcile believers to himself forever. John 19 ended with Jesus's body being buried. Now, in John 20, Jesus's resurrection from the dead will prove that his work on the cross has been effective.

The chapter opens during a quiet morning on the first day of the week, as Mary Magdalene visits the tomb where Jesus has been buried (20:1). Finding the stone rolled back from the tomb's entrance, Mary quickly goes to inform Peter and John that someone has taken Jesus's body (20:2). When Peter and John then race to the tomb, John arrives first; he sees linen cloths inside but doesn't enter (20:3–5). After Peter arrives, they enter the tomb together but find no body (20:6–7). John tells us that, at this moment, he himself "saw" and "believed" that Jesus had been raised from the dead (20:8). As Peter and John both begin to understand the Scriptures' teaching concerning Jesus's death and resurrection, they leave the tomb and return to their homes (20:9–10).

In John 20:11, however, we find that Mary Magdalene has gone back to the tomb; and now she remains there weeping. After a brief visit from two angels (20:12–13), Mary becomes the first person to meet the risen Lord (20:14–18). At first, she does not recognize that it is Jesus (vv. 14–16), but as he speaks, she sees that it is truly him. He instructs Mary to tell his "brothers" that he will soon be ascending to the Father; the passage ends with Mary bearing clear witness to having seen the physically risen Christ (vv. 17–18). Jesus, who had been betrayed and crucified, has now been raised—truly, physically, and victoriously! The Savior who died to save sinners will soon ascend to his Father in order to reign and to send forth the Spirit in power to his people.

Read John 20:1–18.

GETTING STARTED

1. What theories have you heard that try to explain away Jesus Christ's true, physical resurrection from the dead?

2. Which do you think about more: Jesus's death or his resurrection? Why? What makes it clear that these two things are equally important parts of Jesus's saving work?

The Greatest Comedy, pg. 625

What kind of story . . . is the gospel of Jesus and the cross told in John chapter 19? The answer is found in chapter 20, where the death of Jesus is seen not as a tragedy but as a comedy. . . . The greatest of all comedies is the story recounted in John chapter 20, the story of the resurrection of Jesus Christ and the victory he won over the greatest of our enemies—sin, judgment, sorrow, and death.

OBSERVING THE TEXT

3. How do the opening verses of John 20 make it clear that Mary, Peter, and John all expect Jesus to still be dead? What details indicate that Jesus's resurrection comes as an absolute surprise to his followers?

4. How do Mary, John, and Peter each react to the empty tomb? Who is given the important role of bearing first witness to Jesus's resurrection, and what do you think is significant and surprising about this?

5. What signs of deepening faith do you see in this passage?

UNDERSTANDING THE TEXT

6. When Mary Magdalene discovers that the tomb is empty, what is her immediate conclusion (20:1–2)? In what sense is this conclusion logical? What does it reveal about her?

7. What does John do to emphasize the fact that Jesus is truly not inside the tomb when Peter and John arrive (20:3–7)?

8. What do you think it means that John believes that Jesus has been resurrected (20:8) without understanding the Scripture that has foretold this (20:9–10)?

9. What question do the angels ask Mary when she returns to the garden (20:11–13)? What initial response does she give to Jesus—and what causes her response to change (20:14–16)?

10. What instructions does Jesus give to Mary, and what news does she then share (20:17)?

11. What evidence does John give that Jesus is physically present and alive?

BIBLE CONNECTIONS

12. In Romans 4:25, Paul says that Jesus was "raised for our justification"—
    look at verse 5 of that chapter for context, as well. What does Paul mean
    by saying this?

13. Read 1 Corinthians 15:20–26. What does the resurrection of Jesus
    mean for those who believe in him, according to Paul? What exactly
    does Paul mean when he describes Jesus's resurrection as the "firstfruits"
    of all who put their faith in him?

The Necessity of the Resurrection, pg. 632
Note that John refers not merely to the Bible's teaching of Jesus'
resurrection, but to the Scripture's witness to the *necessity* of the
resurrection. . . . It was necessary on Jesus' part that he should rise
from the grave, so that he might triumph over his and our enemies, that
his gospel claims might be vindicated, and that the Father's acceptance
of his atoning blood should be proved.

THEOLOGY CONNECTIONS

14. Answer 52 of the Westminster Larger Catechism explains that "Christ was exalted in his resurrection, in that, not having seen corruption in death (of which it was not possible for him to be held), and having the very same body in which he suffered, with the essential properties thereof (but without mortality, and other common infirmities belonging to this life), really united to his soul, he rose again from the dead the third day by his own power." What aspect of human death did Jesus *not* experience—and why is this important?

15. Many biblical scholars and theologians have described Jesus's resurrection as God the Father's stamp of approval on the atoning work he performed on the cross; it validates Jesus's sacrifice and declares that justice has been done and that the punishment for sin has been paid. What would keep us from being sure of this if Jesus had remained dead?

The Firstfruits, pg. 632

The disciples would learn the full biblical significance of the resurrection under Jesus' teaching of the Scriptures during the days that followed. Then they would learn that Jesus' resurrection was merely the first of a great multitude. Christ was raised as "the firstfruits of those who have fallen asleep" (1 Cor. 15:20).

APPLYING THE TEXT

16. What details from John's account of Jesus's resurrection strengthen your confidence in its historicity and reliability?

17. What assurance does Jesus's resurrection give you about his atoning work—and about what lies ahead for you, in the future, if you trust in him?

18. Reread the instructions that Jesus gives to Mary, as well as her response to them, in 20:17–18. Do these instructions have any application to you, as well? What would it look like for you to emulate Mary?

PRAYER PROMPT

Jesus is alive! Today, thank God for the resurrection's glorious implications and for the hope it gives to every sinner who looks to him with saving faith. Rejoice because Jesus has fully paid the price for your sin and has conquered death itself—and because he is the firstfruits of all who will one day rise in him. As you place your faith in Jesus Christ, ask God to keep you mindful of the reality of your own future resurrection.

LESSON 12

BELIEVING WITHOUT SEEING

John 20:19–31

THE BIG PICTURE

Now that he has recounted Jesus's initial post-resurrection appearance to Mary Magdalene in the garden, John now records two more of the encounters Jesus has with his disciples. The risen Christ is preparing to send his disciples to be his witnesses. Those who have seen him in the flesh will bring the message of salvation to many who will believe without seeing, place their faith in the Son of God, and receive life in his name.

On the first day of the week, Jesus enters a locked room to join his disciples (20:19). Showing them his hands and feet, he declares that he is sending them out, just as he himself has been sent by the Father (20:20–21). Jesus then breathes on his disciples, telling them to receive the Holy Spirit and granting them the message of forgiveness that they will share with men and women (20:22–23).

John then introduces us to Thomas. After missing Jesus's first appearance to the group, he stubbornly insists that he will not accept the reality of his resurrection unless he sees Jesus for himself and touches his wounds (20:24–25). Jesus graciously reappears to his disciples eight days later, and he invites Thomas to touch his hands and side—and to believe (20:26–27). After Thomas expresses his joyful and wholehearted belief, Jesus blesses all who will go on to believe in him, in the generations to come, even though they cannot see him (20:28–29).

The chapter concludes with this gospel's well-known purpose statement (20:30–31). Although John could have included much, much more material in his gospel, he carefully selected all that he needed in order to demonstrate that "Jesus is the Christ, the Son of God," so that the reader—you—might believe in him and find life.

Read John 20:19–31.

GETTING STARTED

1. What kinds of proof do some people claim to require before they will give themselves fully to God? What responses have you seen people give after hearing evidence for Christian beliefs?

2. The Bible is God's living Word. Are you tempted to read it as anything else—and, if so, as what? How does the way that you read Scripture impact how you respond to it?

The Sayings after Christ's Resurrection, pg. 655

Preachers have long celebrated the seven sayings of Jesus spoken on the cross, sometimes referring to these as the last words of our Lord. That description is misleading, however, since Jesus had much to say after he rose from the grave. . . . These are all vitally important sayings of the Lord, all the more so because of their having been spoken in the period after Christ's resurrection.

OBSERVING THE TEXT

3. What evidence does John give us in this passage that Jesus's pre-resurrection body and post-resurrection body are the same—and that Jesus is the same person?

4. Now that Jesus has risen from the dead, what instructions does he give to his disciples? What differences do you see between these instructions and what he was teaching them during the Last Supper?

5. In what way does Jesus demonstrate grace and patience in this passage? What instruction do we get from Jesus (and from John) in the passage about the way we are supposed to respond to the events that this gospel records for us?

God Alone Forgives Sins, pg. 669
Roman Catholicism sees this statement [John 20:23] as establishing a special priesthood possessing the authority to pronounce the absolution of sins. . . . Opposing this doctrine is the Protestant teaching that God alone has authority to forgive sins, that God has not committed this special authority to the church and its clergy, and that what the church receives here is the authority to proclaim the forgiveness of sins through faith in Christ and his gospel.

UNDERSTANDING THE TEXT

6. What does John 20:19 imply about Jesus's resurrection body? What reaction do the disciples have, in 20:20, to seeing him? What does Jesus tell his disciples about the role they will have in the days to come (20:21–22)?

7. What does Jesus do, in 20:22, to begin to fulfill the promises he made to his disciples before his death? What does his statement in 20:23 imply about the role the apostles have of preaching the gospel of the forgiveness of sins that is available through Jesus Christ?

8. What does John tell us that Thomas says in response to the news of Jesus's resurrection (20:24–25)? What does he say will have to happen in order for him to believe it? What similarities do you see between his attitude and the attitude that many people today have regarding God?

9. How does Thomas react when he comes face-to-face with Jesus (20:26–28)?

10. What word of blessing does Jesus speak in John 12:29, and to whom does this blessing apply?

11. What words does John use to describe Jesus in his purpose statement in 20:30–31? What do we learn from the fact that John's gospel does not include all the signs that Jesus performed?

BIBLE CONNECTIONS

12. Read Acts 13:38–39—a portion of the sermon Paul delivers to the Jews of Antioch in Pisidia. ("This man," in those verses, refers to Jesus.) What do these verses add to your understanding of the statement Jesus makes in John 20:23?

13. Hebrews tells us that faith is "the assurance of things hoped for, the conviction of things not seen" (Heb. 11:1). What does Jesus say to affirm this definition of faith when he contrasts it with Thomas's? What makes it particularly important for believers today to understand and embrace this definition of faith?

THEOLOGY CONNECTIONS

14. John 20:23 is a hotly debated verse; in it, Jesus speaks of a kind of authority he has given his disciples to forgive the sins of others—as well as to withhold forgiveness from them. Roman Catholics understand this verse as describing an authority that the church has—along with the ordained priesthood—to grant forgiveness to people who confess their sins and practice penance. How would you demonstrate that this teaching is inconsistent with the message of the Bible? What actual authority is Jesus granting to his followers in this verse—and how do we know that this authority extends to any believer who proclaims the message of the gospel?

15. The Westminster Confession of Faith notes that saving faith in Jesus is "ordinarily" brought about by the "ministry of the Word" (14.1). With that being the case, what is extraordinary about the path that Thomas takes? What does Jesus say to invoke this path that will be taken "ordinarily" by generations of believers to come?

APPLYING THE TEXT

16. What tempts you to feel doubt, even though you are walking with the Lord—and have there been particular times in your life when you were particularly vulnerable to doubt? What do God's Word and his people offer us when we are experiencing doubt?

Seek God and You Will Find Him, pg. 683

Do you have conditions and demands—things that you must see—before you will consider believing in Jesus? Jesus might or might not answer them in the way that you desire, but he will reveal himself to you personally if you will seek him through his Word. . . . It is through his Word that Jesus stands before us today, calling us to faith with a self-disclosure that is just as real and powerful as that which brought Thomas to his knees and with a special blessing for those of us who believe.

17. What does this passage's depiction of Jesus sending his disciples mean for you as his follower today? When you talk about the gospel with others, what emphasis do you give to the forgiveness of sins that is available in his name? Is there anything this passage is challenging you to do differently?

18. What encouragement should you take from the blessing that Jesus promises will come to those who believe without having seen him (20:29)?

PRAYER PROMPT

As you conclude this lesson, ask God to help you to respond to John's gospel in the way that John, and the Holy Spirit, intend: by putting saving belief in the Son of God so that you may have life in his name. Thank your Savior God for the hope he has given you of receiving resurrection life through Jesus, who now lives and reigns at his right hand in heaven. Pray for strength and courage so that you can bear witness to the risen Christ and joyfully proclaim the forgiveness of sins that will be granted to all who believe in his name.

LESSON 13

FEEDING THE SHEEP

John 21:1–25

THE BIG PICTURE

In our study, we have encountered events and interactions that are unique to John's gospel—and we will see this again in its final chapter. As Jesus prepares to return to the Father, he reveals himself to some of his disciples in order to strengthen their faith, encourage their hearts, and equip them to serve him and one another.

A group of the disciples have returned to Galilee to wait obediently for further instructions from Jesus and to learn what the next steps of their call to gospel ministry will be, and they decide to go fishing in the meantime (21:1–3). After Jesus appears to them on the shore and directs them to a miraculously large catch of fish, Peter hurls himself into the water out of sheer excitement and swims to join Jesus (21:4–8). In the tender and affectionate scene that follows, Jesus invites the disciples to share a meal of fish after he cooks it over a fire for them; John notes that this is now the third time Jesus has revealed himself to his disciples following his resurrection (21:9–14).

John's narrative then shows us what seems to be a private conversation between Jesus and Peter (21:15–19). Jesus asks Peter three times to affirm his love for him and, each time Peter does, tells him to "feed [Jesus's] sheep." Peter is "grieved" by the threefold repetition of Jesus's question, which recalls his own threefold denial of Jesus on the eve of the crucifixion. Yet, in a spirit of loving forgiveness, Jesus is reaffirming Peter and preparing him to deliver bold and costly witness for the gospel in the months and years ahead.

As the chapter, and the entire book, come to a close, John recounts a question that Peter asks Jesus about him (21:20–23). He concludes his gospel by attesting to the trustworthiness of its testimony and noting that much more could be recorded about Jesus Christ—so much, in fact, that the whole world could not contain it all (21:24–25).

Read John 21:1–25.

GETTING STARTED

1. What effects can shame have on our minds and hearts? In what ways can both shame and regret threaten to paralyze us from obeying, from witnessing, or from confidently serving God and others?

2. How do your struggles with comparing yourself to other Christians, and wondering why your life doesn't look more like theirs, manifest themselves? What makes such comparisons dangerous?

"Follow Me," pg. 715

In concluding his gospel, John provides Jesus' own definition of saving faith: "Follow me" (21:19). James Montgomery Boice observes that these words "are a reminder that Christianity is Christ, not just believing in some abstract sense, but believing in him to the point of turning our back on all else to follow him."

OBSERVING THE TEXT

3. What physical details does John emphasize in this passage—and especially in its opening scene? Why do you think he paints this opening scene so vividly for his readers?

4. What does Jesus do in this passage to demonstrate his gentleness, grace, and patience? Where do you see him correcting, rebuking, and instructing his disciples?

5. What strikes you about John's conclusion to his gospel (21:24–25)? What does he emphasize as he ends the book?

UNDERSTANDING THE TEXT

6. In what way does John 21:1–3 introduce the scene that opens the chapter? What questions might we still have about how well the disciples understand the resurrection, about their faith in Jesus, and about how ready they are to share the gospel?

7. What final sign does Jesus perform to demonstrate his power and identity (21:4–6)? What is Peter's immediate reaction to the sign—and what does this tell us about his attitude regarding, and his relationship with, Jesus (21:7–8)?

8. What happens in 21:9–14? How does this scene demonstrate the fact that, even though he has a resurrection body, Jesus is still truly human? What encouragement should we derive from the way Jesus treats the disciples, even though they so recently abandoned him?

9. What is the significance of the question that Jesus repeats to Peter in 21:15–19? What is he communicating to Peter through this interaction, and what does this tell us about how Jesus responds to believers who fall short as they seek to follow him?

Resurrection Courage, pg. 695

Now the disciples had gathered in open allegiance to Jesus, presenting themselves in the region of Jesus' most public and notorious works. No longer did Peter think of denying his Lord; no longer were the other disciples scurrying for a place of cover. What can account for this renewal of courage and faith other than the fact of Jesus' resurrection, of which they had now become witnesses?

10. What seems to lie behind Peter's question about John (21:20–21)? How does Jesus answer his question—and what rumor begins to spread as a result (21:22–23)? What clarification does John give us about it?

11. What does John affirm about himself and his gospel (21:24)? What do we learn about the extent of the work Jesus has done during his mere thirty-three years on earth (21:25)?

BIBLE CONNECTIONS

12. Read Matthew 28:10–11, in which Jesus tells the women who have encountered him to pass on instructions to the disciples. What better understanding do these instructions give us regarding the beginning of John 21? (Note that the Sea of Tiberias is another name for the Sea of Galilee.)

13. Look at 1 Peter 1:3–9. What themes does Peter introduce as he begins this letter? How can he be said to have experienced some of what he is describing in these verses, and what evidence do you see of his growth in Christ?

THEOLOGY CONNECTIONS

14. The warm and affectionate scene that takes place as Jesus eats breakfast with his disciples around the fire on the beach gives us hints of what awaits us in the new heaven and new earth. What does it indicate about our own resurrection bodies? What can we perhaps anticipate about the fellowship we will have with our risen and reigning Savior when we finally see him face to face?

15. According to answer 36 of the Westminster Shorter Catechism, the "benefits" that justification, sanctification, and adoption bring are "assurance of God's love, peace of conscience, joy in the Holy Spirit, increase of grace, and perseverance therein to the end." In what ways do you see the disciples beginning to experience these benefits in John 21?

APPLYING THE TEXT

16. Consider how you might react if you suddenly encountered Jesus and had breakfast with him. Would your reaction be any different from the one the disciples have in John 21? In what ways might thinking about this scene help you to deepen your relationship with Christ even now when you can not see him?

17. What encouragement can you take from this passage regarding the service that you can offer to God, despite your own weaknesses and failures?

18. What does this passage teach you about being content with the specific calling that you have received from God, even if it is a difficult one? What happens when we become too preoccupied with the roles and callings of others?

The Character of Christ's Church, pg. 695

In this list of names [in John 21:2] we are reminded of the character of Christ's church. As it was then, so has the church always consisted of those who have been spiritual failures and nonentities. This list of names is headed by one who denied his Lord and another who was determined in disbelief. . . . They were now gathered and unified as sinners cleansed of their sins by Christ's atoning death and renewed by faith in their resurrected Lord.

PRAYER PROMPT

John's gospel ends by giving us hope through its reminder that the disciples, who will go on to be sent out as witnesses to the crucified and risen Lord, had to be *saved* by faith, themselves, in this same Savior before they could proclaim him. Thank God, now, for the grace he has shown you through Christ—the Savior who died for your sins and now graciously invites you, as well, to follow him and serve as a witness to him. Praise God for giving you the privilege of being able to join in the same pattern of gospel proclamation that the apostles began: the pattern of saved sinners pointing others to the Savior!

Jon Nielson is senior pastor of Christ Presbyterian Church in Wheaton, Illinois, and the author of *Bible Study: A Student's Guide*, among other books. He has served in pastoral positions at several churches in Illinois—including Holy Trinity Church in Chicago, College Church in Wheaton, and Spring Valley Presbyterian Church in Roselle—and as director of training for the Charles Simeon Trust.

Richard D. Phillips (MDiv, Westminster Theological Seminary; DD, Greenville Presbyterian Theological Seminary) is the senior minister of Second Presbyterian Church of Greenville, South Carolina. He is a council member of the Alliance of Confessing Evangelicals and of The Gospel Coalition and chairman of the Philadelphia Conference on Reformed Theology.

Did you enjoy this Bible study? Consider writing a review online.
The authors appreciate your feedback!

Or write to P&R at editorial@prpbooks.com with your comments.
We'd love to hear from you.

P&R PUBLISHING'S COMPANION COMMENTARY

Richard Phillips's two-volume commentary on John reflects the Reformed Expository Commentary series's commitment to thorough, Calvinistic, redemptive-historical, and expositional teaching of the biblical text. Discover the apostle John's chief focus on the deity of Christ, the gospel witness of the church, and salvation through faith in Jesus. Although scholarly, it explains doctrines lucidly, communicates in nontechnical language, and applies each passage to the reader's life.

The Reformed Expository Commentary (REC) series is accessible to both pastors and lay readers. Each volume in the series provides exposition that gives careful attention to the biblical text, is doctrinally Reformed, focuses on Christ through the lens of redemptive history, and applies the Bible to our contemporary setting.

Praise for the Reformed Expository Commentary Series

"Well-researched and well-reasoned, practical and pastoral, shrewd, solid, and searching." —**J. I. Packer**

"A rare combination of biblical insight, theological substance, and pastoral application." —**Al Mohler**

"Here, rigorous expository methodology, nuanced biblical theology, and pastoral passion combine." —**R. Kent Hughes**